The Railway

by Galadriel Watson

WEIGL EDUCATIONAL PUBLISHERS

Published by Weigl Educational Publishers Limited
6325-10 Street SE
Calgary, Alberta
Canada T2H 2Z9
Web site: www.weigl.com

Library and Archives Canada Cataloguing in Publication Data

Watson, Galadriel Findlay
      The railway / Galadriel Watson.

(Early Canadian life)
Includes index.
ISBN 1-55388-061-7 (bound).--ISBN 1-55388-095-1 (pbk.)

     1. Railroads--Canada--History--Juvenile literature. 2. Frontier and pioneer life--Canada--Juvenile literature. I. Title. II. Series: Early Canadian life (Calgary, Alta.)

HE2808.W38 2004   j385'.0971   C2004-904098-7

Printed and bound in the United States of America
1 2 3 4 5 6 7 8 9 0 09 08 07 06 05 04

We acknowledge the financial support of the Government of Canada through the Book Publishing Industry Development Program (BPIDP) for our publishing activities.

Photograph Credits
Every reasonable effort has been made to trace ownership and to obtain permission to reprint copyright material. The publishers would be pleased to have any errors or omissions brought to their attention so that they may be corrected in subsequent printings.
Cover: Glenbow Archives: main (NA-659-18), **Canadian Pacific Railway** background; **Alberta Railway Museum**: page 23L; **Barrett & MacKay Photography Inc.**: pages 4, 5, 8, 14B, 22; **Ellen Bryan**: pages 10, 14T, 15M, 15B, 23R; **Canada Science and Technology Museum, CSTM/CN Collection**: pages 11 (no. 15262), 17 (no. CN000456), 18 (no. 03187); **Canadian Pacific Railway**: pages 9, 20; **Glenbow Archives**: pages 13T (NA-1753-22), 14M (NA-1167-10), 15T (NA-1313-3), 16 (NA-1167-12); **McCord Museum of Canadian History, Montreal**: page 13B (M20982 Watch); **National Archives of Canada**: pages 1 (PA-4478), 6 (PA-4478), 19 (C-17630A); **Photos.com**: pages 3T, 3B, 12; **Saskatchewan Archives Board**: page 7 (R-A2319).

Project Coordinator
Tina Schwartzenberger

Design
Janine Vangool

Layout
Jeff Brown

Substantive Editor
Janice L. Redlin

Copy Editor
Frances Purslow

Photo Researcher
Ellen Bryan

Contents

Introduction

In its early years, Canada was a collection of scattered communities. Later, railways were built to connect these communities. Canadians could travel and communicate more easily. Many railway passengers were **immigrants** moving to Canada's West. Other passengers were travelling to see the Rocky Mountains. Some people travelled from western Canada to visit their families in eastern Canada. Railways took Canadians across the country.

Roads in early Canada were very poor. Many waterways were frozen for up to 5 months each year. People were excited about the railways, which offered a new way to travel across the country.

4

The size of a railway station depended on its importance. Stations in cities and towns were large. Often, these stations had living space, offices, and, sometimes, a restaurant.

Telegraph lines were built alongside railway tracks. The telegraph brought news from far away. Railway stations became important centres. In eastern Canada, railways linked towns and cities. In western Canada, towns often grew around railway stations. For example, Calgary, Vancouver, and Winnipeg grew around railway stations.

Did you know:

Canada had a very simple railway in the 1720s. The railway consisted of wooden rails and horse-drawn carts. The railway carried building stones to the Fortress of Louisbourg on Cape Breton Island.

From Sea to Sea

Canadians were excited about the Canadian Pacific Railway (CPR) that would link Canada from sea to sea. This railway made the provinces of British Columbia, New Brunswick, and Nova Scotia decide to join Canada. Without a railway, these provinces did not feel connected to the rest of Canada. The railway gave them a way to communicate with the rest of the country. The railway also gave Canadians a way to transport goods across Canada. The Canadian Pacific Railway stretched 3,200 kilometres across the country. At the time, it was the world's longest railway.

On May 23, 1887, the Canadian Pacific Railway line was extended to Vancouver, British Columbia. The Port Moody-based locomotive 374 pulled the first train into Vancouver.

The final spike completed the Canadian Pacific Railway in 1885. The total cost to build the railway was $150 million.

Building the railway was hard work. Surveyors measured the land to find the best routes for the train to travel. Grading gangs cleared trees from the route. Workers called navvies built the **roadbed**. Tracklayers used iron spikes to fasten the wooden **ties**. Bridge gangs built bridges and **trestles**. Dynamite crews blasted through rock to make tunnels. The CPR was completed in 1885. It took 14 years to survey and build the railway. Surveyors spent 10 years finding a route across Canada.

Did you know:

Before the Canadian Pacific Railway was built, Canada had many short railways. The Champlain and St. Lawrence Railroad, for example, was less than 25 kilometres long.

First-hand account:

On November 7, 1885, workers from eastern and western Canada met in Craigellachie, B.C. When the final spike was hammered in to complete the railway, it was a joyous occasion.

Finally, there remained but one more spike to be driven. It was partly driven in and a hammer was given to Sir Donald Smith to drive it home.... Everybody cheered; the locomotives whistled and shrieked; several short speeches were made; hands were shaken.

Steam Engines

A train's engine is called a locomotive. In the early days, steam powered train engines. The **tender** carried fuel, such as coal or wood, and water to power the steam engine. A worker called a fireman shovelled the fuel into the fire in the engine to heat the water. The boiling water produced steam. The steam pushed the train's pistons back and forth. Pistons moved the driving rods, which turned the large driving wheels. These wheels turned the other wheels that moved the train along the tracks.

Train locomotives were often called "iron horses."

The large steel wheels attached to the engine are the driving wheels. Without driving wheels, the train would not move.

Trains also had safety features. A smokestack at the front of the train sent smoke high above the train. The smokestack kept sparks from flying out and lighting grass— or passengers' hats—on fire. The train also used a bell and whistle to warn people and animals along the tracks that the train was approaching. A headlight helped the engineer see at night. The shining light also warned people and animals that the train was coming.

Did you know:

A sand dome on the locomotive held sand. The sand was sprinkled on the track to provide traction, or grip, for the train's wheels when the track was icy.

First-hand account:

In the early 1800s, surveyors pushed through thick forest. One newspaper commented on the coming of the railway:

The days of stage coaches have come to an end, and everywhere is to be heard the snorting of the iron horse, and the shrill blast of the steam whistle warning the thoughtless of the danger if they have ventured upon its path.

9

All Aboard!

Train passengers chose the type of train car they wanted for their journey. A colonist car was the most basic type of car. It had hard wooden benches and uncomfortable sleeping platforms, called berths. Passengers had to cook their own meals. They also had to bring their own blankets. There were no bathrooms on the train, so passengers had to wait for the train to stop at a railway station.

Most passengers travelling in colonist cars were settlers moving west.

Passengers travelling first class could pay a small fee to use the parlour car. The car had a smoking room and comfortable seats.

A coach car was for short trips. Passengers could buy newspapers and candy from a person called a candy butcher during the trip. A second-class sleeper car offered more comfort. People called porters helped passengers settle in their berths. Curtains closed for privacy while passengers slept.

A first-class sleeper was the ultimate luxury. Walls of mahogany wood, stained-glass windows, and carpet surrounded the passengers. Bathrooms offered hot and cold water. Many homes at the time did not even have hot and cold water. The dining car served **gourmet** food.

First-hand account:

Privileged passengers rode on the **cowcatcher**. One rider, Prime Minister John A. Macdonald's wife, Agnes, described it like this:

So steady was the engine that I felt perfectly secure and the only damage we did from Ottawa to the sea was to kill a lovely little fat pig.

Tools of the Railway

Several tools made a railway worker's job and a passenger's trip easy. Some of these tools are still used today.

Hand Signals

Workers on distant parts of a train needed to communicate with each other. They used hand signals. A hand held high above the head meant to release the brakes to slow or stop the train. A hand swung across the track meant to stop. At night, workers held lanterns so they could see each other's signals.

Rotary Snowplough

A train could not drive through snow piled over the tracks, The train stopped while crew members, and sometimes even passengers, shovelled the snow away. In 1869, J. W. Elliot, a Toronto dentist invented the rotary snowplough. The locomotive pushed the snowplough, which could cut through deep snow drifts and plow snow off the track.

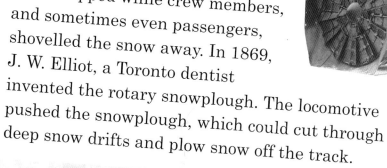

Standard Time

Before the nineteenth century ended, every town chose its own time. A Canadian train worker and passenger named Sandford Fleming invented Standard Time. He divided the world into 24 time zones. All the clocks in a time zone were set to the same time. This system was adopted around the world. near the end of the nineteenth century. Standard Time helped passengers board their trains on time.

A Day in the Life

Many workers had special jobs that helped the train move. Here is what a typical day may have been like on a train in early Canada.

7:00 a.m.

A person called a dispatcher gave train orders to the station agent. The engineer and conductor received the train orders from the station agent. The orders told the engineer and conductor when to leave, how fast to drive, and when to stop. The station agent was the person who sold tickets to passengers.

9:00 a.m.

"All aboard!" the conductor yelled. The conductor was the train's boss and told everyone else what they had to do. Inside the train, porters greeted the passengers and showed them to their seats. The engineer drove the train. The engineer decided how much steam the engine needed to increase speed and decided when to apply the brakes to slow the train down.

10:00 a.m.

The train stopped at the first railway station. Some passengers got off the train, and others boarded. When the train started again, the fireman saw that the fuel in the tender was running low. The fireman climbed on top of the tender to add fuel. The conductor went to the caboose, or the back of the train. The conductor or a brakeman climbed into the cupola, a glass room on the top of the caboose, to watch for the engineer's hand signals.

noon

The water was running low. The train stopped to stock up on fuel and water at a refuelling stop along the tracks. Many passengers went to the dining car for lunch. The chief steward, who supervised the cooks and waiters, greeted the passengers and seated them at tables. The train sped past a sectionman, who patrolled a section of track every day. The sectionman fixed any damage and put out fires caused by flying sparks. The sectionman watched for objects along the track. If an object could not be moved, the sectionman warned the train to stop.

1:00 p.m.

The train reached its divisional point. At this place, trains turned around. A switchman moved the train onto a sidetrack. This allowed another train coming from the opposite direction to pass by. On the sidetrack, the brakeman uncoupled, or unhooked, the train from the locomotive. The locomotive was turned around, and coupled, or hooked, to another set of cars. It was now time for the crew to return home.

9:00 p.m.

The train returned to the same railway station it left earlier that day. The passengers left the train. The crew parked the locomotive in the roundhouse, or repair shop. While the locomotive was in the roundhouse, mechanics fixed any broken parts.

Dangers and Disasters

Although train travel was generally safe, there were some dangers. Canada's first railway accident occurred in 1837. A train derailed, or fell off the track, when it hit a team of oxen.

Sometimes the engineer lost control of the train when driving down a steep hill. The "runaway train" had to be switched to a runaway lane to slow down. Sometimes engineers raced trains that were driving on side-by-side tracks.

In 1891, a train travelling from Great Falls, Montana, to Canada derailed. Water washed away soil from under the track, causing an accident.

Often, after heavy snowfalls or avalanches, passengers were expected to help shovel snow off the tracks. Trains could not move until the tracks were clear.

Brakemen had a dangerous job. Before air brakes were invented in 1869, brakemen had to run along the top of the cars to apply the brakes. They had to run in all kinds of weather, even when the train was travelling at top speed. Also, if a brakeman waited too long to insert the hook and chain when coupling cars, the brakeman could be crushed. Avalanches were another danger. Strong wooden tunnels, called snowsheds, were built in some areas to keep snow off the track.

First-hand account:

Workers faced many hazards while building the railway. Workers faced accidents, horrible weather, wild animals, and forest fires.

The fire burned for days. It was pretty hot, and the smoke was bad for a time, but we, our camp outfit, and supplies came through safely—also our horses, which we had driven to a small meadow close to the river. But some of the men and teams working on the line were burned.

Special Trains

Some trains carried special **freight** and passengers. Starting in the 1890s, silk trains delivered raw silk from Vancouver to mills in New York and New Jersey. The cargo was very valuable and spoiled quickly. The trains carried guards, travelled at very fast speeds, and only stopped when necessary. Silk trains had the right of way over all other trains. This meant that other trains had to move off the track to allow silk trains to pass. Other special trains brought dentists, doctors, and schoolteachers to isolated communities.

Ships brought silk to Vancouver, B.C. Trains carried the silk from Vancouver to mills in the United States. A trainload of silk was worth as much as $2.5 million.

Almost 3,000 soldiers travelled on trains from Ontario, Quebec, and Nova Scotia to Saskatchewan in 1885.

Trains carried soldiers for the first time in 1885. The Canadian Pacific Railway's tracks were not built in some places. The soldiers had to get off the train and walk through snow and ice to get to the next section of track. Still, the soldiers made their trip in 9 days. They travelled from Toronto, Ontario, to what is now central Saskatchewan. Before the railway, the trip would have taken 3 months.

Did you know:

In 1901, the Duke of York travelled through Canada on a special luxury train. Other royal visitors to Canada travelled on trains that had hair salons on board.

First-hand account:

Some trains pulled circuses. One brakeman remembers what it was like travelling with lions:

It was breaking dawn, and those lions started to roar in that close canyon; you wouldn't believe the echoes. I think every billy goat for 100 miles was scared to death!

Railways Past and Present

Many Canadians today rely on underground trains called subways to travel around their cities. Trains transport many items such as lumber, grain, and new cars. The CPR is no longer the longest railway system. With more than 50,000 kilometres of track, the Canadian National Railway system is the longest railway system in North America.

Spitting is **prohibited** in cars, waiting rooms, and on platforms.

Passengers are asked to keep their feet off the seats.

Due to the fire hazard, smoking in sleeping car berth sections is prohibited.

Today, the Canadian Pacific Railway has more than 46,000 railway cars. These railway cars transport goods across North America.

Then

Early Railways

- The locomotive is fuelled by steam
- The last car is a caboose
- Train crews use hand signals to communicate with each other
- Brakemen run atop cars to apply the brakes and couple and uncouple cars manually

- An engineer drives the train
- Railways bring travellers from around the world to the Rocky Mountains
- The Canadian Pacific Railway runs across Canada
- Passengers sleep in berths

Now

Today's Railways

- The locomotive is fuelled by diesel
- Cabooses are no longer used
- Train crews use radios to communicate with each other
- Railway cars are coupled and uncoupled automatically

DIAGRAM

There are many differences between pioneer railways and railways operating today. There are some similarities between the two as well. The diagram on the left compares these similarities and differences. Copy the diagram in your notebook. Try to think of other similarities and differences to add to your diagram.

As you can see by the diagram, railways today have some things in common with railways 100 years ago.

Preserving the Past

Although steam engines are no longer in general use, people can still see these locomotives. Some steam engines offer rides in Canada's museums and historic parks. The map shows some of these railways. Can you think of any others that could be added to the map?

1 **Revelstoke Railway Museum**
Revelstoke, BC

2 **Alberta Railway Museum**
Edmonton, AB

3 **Saskatchewan Railway Museum**
Saskatoon, SK

4 **Transcona Historical Museum**
Winnipeg, MB

5 **Smith Falls Railway Museum**
Smith Falls, ON

6 **Canadian Railway Museum**
Saint-Constant, QB

7 **McAdam Railway Station**
McAdam, NB

8 **Elmira Railway Station**
Charlottetown, PEI

9 **Sydney and Louisbourg Railway Museum**
Cape Breton, NS

10 **Railway Coastal Museum**
St. John's, NF

11 **Miles Canyon Historic Railway Society**
Whitehorse, YT

12 **Steam Locomotives No. 2023 and 2024**
Heritage Park Historical Village, Calgary, AB

Alberta Railway Museum

Heritage Park
Historical Village

Glossary

Cowcatcher: a part on the front of a train that moved objects and animals off the tracks

Freight: goods carried by railways over land, through air by airplanes, or over water by ships

Gourmet: high-quality food that is expensive, rare, or difficult to prepare

Immigrants: people who moved to a new country

Prohibited: not allowed

Roadbed: the foundation, or base, that a road or railway is built on

Telegraph: a method of communicating by sending electric impulses through wires

Tender: the railway car attached to the steam engine

Ties: the wooden beams of railway tracks that the rails sit on

Trestles: a framework that holds up a railway bridge

Index